A Satie Flute Album

Arranged by Trevor Wye

FLUTE

NOVELLO PUBLISHING LIMITED
8/9 Frith Street, London W1D 3JB

Order No: NOV 120554

CONTENTS

page 1 Préambule
from *Cinq Grimaces*

3 Fanfaronnade
from *Cinq Grimaces*

4 Pour Sortir
from *Cinq Grimaces*

5 Gnossienne
No. 1 from *Trois Gnossiennes*

9 Le Picadilly
Marche

11 Airs à faire fuir
No. 2 from *Pièces Froides I*

13 Trois Gymnopédies

A SATIE FLUTE ALBUM

FLUTE

Arranged by
TREVOR WYE

1 PRÉAMBULE
from Cinq Grimaces

2 FANFARONNADE
from Cinq Grimaces

3 POUR SORTIR

from Cinq Grimaces

4 GNOSSIENNE

No. 1 from Trois Gnossiennes

Postulez en vous-même (*Postulate within yourself*)

Pas à pas (*Step by step*)

Sur la langue (*On the tongue*)

5 LE PICCADILLY

Pas trop vite

Marche

FINE   TRIO

D.C. al Fine

4

6 AIRS À FAIRE FUIR

No. 2 from Pièces Froides I

Modestement

Sans sourciller (Without raising the eyebrows)

A sucer (Sucking)

Dans le plus profond silence (In the most profound silence)

*As no dynamic was given by Satie suggested dynamics have been added by the arranger.

**as left by Satie

7 TROIS GYMNOPÉDIES

Lent et douloureux   I

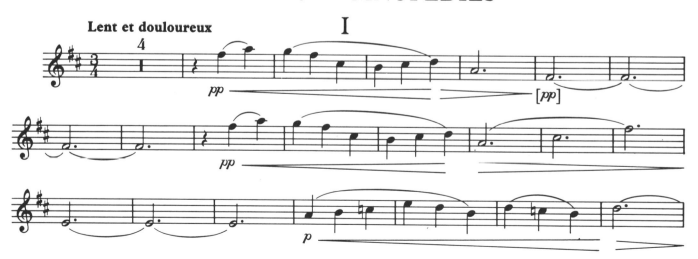

II

Lent et triste

III

Lent et grave

rocess-engraved by Michael L. Rowe

Printed in Great Britain

/07(61957)

A Satie Flute Album

Arranged by Trevor Wye

NOVELLO PUBLISHING LIMITED
8/9 Frith Street, London W1D 3JB

Order No: NOV 120554

Cover by Art & Design Services

This copy may not be sold in France.

CONTENTS

Page 1   Préambule
from *Cinq Grimaces*

3   Fanfaronnade
from *Cinq Grimaces*

4   Pour Sortir
from *Cinq Grimaces*

5   Gnossienne
No. 1 from *Trois Gnossiennes*

9   Le Piccadilly
Marche

11   Airs à faire fuir
No. 2 from *Pièces Froides I*

13   Trois Gymnopédies

Preface

Erik Satie was born in Honfleur, France, of a Scottish mother and French father, in 1866.

His writing, both musical and literary, was most often satirical and led to his work not being taken seriously though it is now widely respected as having an important place in the development of twentieth-century music.

Many of his works contain tongue-in-cheek comments designed to help the performer but not to be read out to the audience!

I hope this volume will help Satie gain more friends amongst flute players.

T.W.

I am indebted to Robert Scott for his help with the piano accompaniment.

T.W.

A SATIE FLUTE ALBUM

Arranged by
TREVOR WYE

1 PRÉAMBULE

from Cinq Grimaces

2 FANFARONNADE

from Cinq Grimaces

Temps de marche

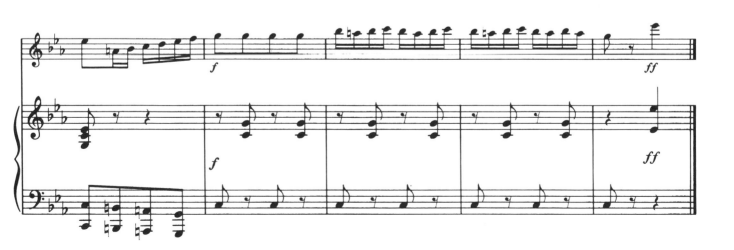

3 POUR SORTIR

from Cinq Grimaces

4 GNOSSIENNE

No. 1 from Trois Gnossiennes

Du bout de la pensée (From the edge of your thoughts)

8

5 LE PICCADILLY

Marche

6 AIRS À FAIRE FUIR

No. 2 from Pièces Froides I

Modestement

col Ped.

Sans sourciller (Without raising the eyebrows)

*As no dynamic was given by Satie suggested dynamics have been added by the arranger.

12

A sucer (Sucking)

Dans le plus profond silence (In the most profound silence)

*as left by Satie

7 TROIS GYMNOPÉDIES

I

II

Lent et triste

18

III

4/07(61957)

Music for Flute

Solo

Gordon Saunders
Eight Traditional Japanese Pieces
Gordon Saunders has selected and transcribed these pieces for tenor recorder solo or flute from the traditional folk music of Japan.

Trevor Wye
Practice Book for the Flute

Volume 1 TONE
Volume 2 TECHNIQUE
Volume 3 ARTICULATION
Volume 4 INTONATION
Volume 5 BREATHING AND SCALES

Flute & Piano

Richard Rodney Bennett
Summer Music *Associated Board Grade VII*

Charles Camilleri
Sonata Antica

Edward Elgar
An Elgar Flute Album *arranged by Trevor Wye*

Gabriel Fauré
A Fauré Flute Album *arranged by Trevor Wye*

James Galway
Showpieces
The Magic Flute of James Galway
Two albums, each containing ten favourite pieces by various composers, arranged for flute and piano by James Galway. Both include photographs and a separate flute part.

Michael Hurd
Sonatina

John McCabe
Portraits *Associated Board Grades V & VI*

Eric Satie
A Satie Flute Album *arranged by Trevor Wye*

Robert Schumann
A Schumann Flute Album *arranged by Trevor Wye*

Gerard Schurmann
Sonatina

604(85)